# FARMHOUSE
# COOKING

# FARMHOUSE COOKING

## Anne Walton

*Illustrated by Henry Brewis*

Bridge Studios
Northumberland
1992

First published in Great Britain in 1992

by Bridge Studios,
   Kirklands,
   The Old Vicarage,
   Scremerston,
   Berwick-upon-Tweed,
   TD15 2RB.

Tel: 0289 302658/330274

ISBN 1 872010 90 3

Cover photograph by Alistair McDonald

Typeset by EMS Phototypesetting, Berwick upon Tweed.

Printed by CP Offset Limited
   Kellaw Road,
   Yarm Road Industrial Estate,
   Darlington,
   County Durham DL1 4YA.
   Telephone (0325) 462315.
   Fax (0325) 462767.

# CONTENTS

To my husband Michael and the rest of my family, who have put up with running our lives around an ever-expanding farm-shop and non-stop activity in the kitchen.

# FOREWORD

Anne Walton can hardly remember a time when she has not been busy in the kitchen. She cooked as a child and coming from a farming family – she has four sisters – her childhood memories are steeped in the family farm and plenty of activity in the farmhouse kitchen.

Anne Walton would be the first to admit that a lot of her cooking skills have been inherited. 'Granny was a marvellous cook as indeed was mother, so much of it has been handed down.'

Thirty years ago she married her husband Michael and moved to Roseden, a farm close to the Cheviot Hills in the heart of Northumberland. However, life as a farmer's wife has its share of ups and downs. It was during one of these downs that seven years ago she dreamed up the idea of starting a farm shop. Everything would be home-made and produced on the farm (with one or two exceptions). Meat, poultry, free-range eggs, bread, cakes and scones, jams, pickles, chutneys and bottled fruit, vegetables and fresh fruit, farm butter and cheese. As a result Anne Walton's passion for farmhouse cooking has gone from strength to strength. Perhaps it is just as well for the popularity of her farmhouse shop means she is frequently up until the early hours preparing and baking for the next day's customers. Her reputation as a cook has spread far and wide and in 1990 she came second in the Farming Woman of the Year Competition which was organised in association with *Farmers Weekly* and the Women's Farming Union.

Anne has three sons and enjoys every minute of what has become a very hectic life but the delights of her farmhouse cooking – the richness of a gamekeeper's wife's fruit cake, a simple cheese scone or a casserole of wood pigeons are what traditional country cooking is all about.

The majority of the recipes in this book have been handed down and a large number have been given to me by various friends over the years and I do not know the origin of them.

The problem with farmers wives as cooks, and very good straightforward cooking has been their success, they rarely weigh anything. I do not say it is thrown in (sometimes it may be) but they are not as accurate as, say, Katie Stewart's recipes, she is noted for her accuracy.

Having been brought up with pounds and ounces, I have set out all the recipes using those measurements. The more modern among you will have to bear with me and convert to metric if you find imperial impossible!

Likewise, oven temperatures are purely instinctive with me and I haven't gone into great detail. Suffice it to say a slow oven is about Gas 1-2/275-300°F/140-150°C, a moderate oven Gas 3-4/325-350°F/160-180°C and a hot oven Gas 7/425°F/220°C.

Seasoning, in the best of recipes, is to one's own taste and I think you will find most of my recipes say so for this very reason.

The handy hints dotted throughout the book are all tried and tested and have been gathered together over the years.

As far as quantities go, most dishes serve four people unless otherwise indicated. However, this is totally dependent on appetite and can only be taken as a rough guide!

Anne Walton

# Soups and Starters

Many of these soups are old-fashioned and meals in themselves but I have put them in for good measure. Many were invented to nourish during the cold bleak winters and often other favourite vegetables can be added to suit family tastes.

You can, of course, experiment, as long as one flavour does not kill another. The basic ingredients are there and soup is one of the easiest courses to prepare.

Quantities are for 4-6 people.

# IMITATION HARE SOUP

*1 lb lean beef (cut off fat, use for frying)*
*1 large onion*
*1 large carrot*
*small quantity of turnip*
*1 oz butter (or dripping, or use fat from meat)*
*1 oz flour*
*2 pints stock*
*6 crushed peppercorns*
*dash of Worcestershire sauce*
*salt*

Fry the onion. Brown the flour in the pan when onion is taken out. Add cold stock.
Cut the meat and vegetables very small and put in saucepan with the stock.
Bring to the boil and simmer for at least 1½ hours.
Make forcemeat balls to go with this soup.

### Forcemeat balls
*1 oz breadcrumbs*
*tablespoon chopped suet*
*mixed herbs*
*small egg to bind*
*a pinch of nutmeg*
*a little zest of lemon*
*salt and pepper*

Mix to a paste with egg and make into small balls.
Liquidise the soup, return to clean pan, put in the forcemeat balls and cook for a further half hour.

# CHICKEN SOUP WITH A DIFFERENCE

*good chicken stock from a small boiling chicken*
*carrots*
*cauliflower*
*parsnip*
*celery*

*green peas*
*salt and black pepper*


Boil the chicken with a bunch of parsley until tender.
Remove meat from the chicken and cut into small pieces.
Put the prepared vegetables into the strained stock.
Season.
Boil until vegetables are cooked then add meat and serve with a sprinkling of parsley.

# VEGETABLE MARROW SOUP

*2 medium onions*
*1 large marrow*
*2 oz fat or oil*
*milk to finish*
*2 pints chicken stock*
*2 oz plain flour*
*salt and several grinds of black pepper*


Chop the onions very finely. Peel and remove seeds from the marrow and cut up.
Melt about 1 oz butter in pan, add onion and marrow and cook with lid on for about 20 minutes. Add stock. Cook until the marrow is tender.
Liquidise, clean out liquidiser with ½ to 1 pint of milk. Return to pan and thicken with remainder of fat mixed with the flour. Stir until the soup boils.
Garnish with chopped parsley.


**Handy hint**
*Fasten a ring pull (from a lemonade can) with a small nail on to paint brush handles to hang them on the wall out of the way. Can (excuse the pun) be used on a number of small household tools.*

# TOMATO & COURGETTE SOUP

*½ lb tomatoes*
*(1 x 15 oz tin of tomatoes if fresh not available)*
*½ lb courgettes*
*2 oz butter*
*1 pint stock*
*1 tablespoon tomato purée (depending upon taste)*
*1 tablespoon sugar*
*bayleaf*
*salt and pepper*
*a little paprika*

Sweat vegetables in butter for 10 minutes, add stock and a little seasoning – more can be added to taste at the end. Add tomato purée and cook for a further 10 – 20 minutes or when vegetables are sufficiently cooked.
Cool and liquidise. Sieve if necessary.
Reheat, adding more sugar and seasoning to taste.

# VEGETABLE SOUP

*2 cups dried peas*
*2 cups split peas*
*2 cups lentils*
*2 cups barley*
*2 leeks*
*2 carrots*
*small quantity of turnip*
*beef stock, about 2 pints – can be thinned as desired*
*salt and pepper*

Soak dried peas overnight. Wash split peas, lentils and barley.
Add all ingredients to stock and simmer gently (adding more stock as required) until everything is completely cooked.
(At one time a piece of beef would be added to the water – instead of using stock – and this would then be used after serving the soup as a main course).

# LEEK AND POTATO SOUP

*1 lb leeks*
*1 lb potatoes*
*small onion*
*stick of celery*
*1 oz butter*
*1 teaspoonful plain flour*
*½ pint milk*
*1 pint stock*
*salt and pepper*

Chop vegetables roughly. Melt the fat and sauté the vegetables in it for five minutes. When the fat is absorbed by the vegetables add the stock, flavouring and seasoning.
Bring to the boil, put a lid on the pan and simmer until the vegetables are cooked. Liquidise and put through a sieve. Mix the flour with a little milk and add to the sieved soup with the rest of the milk (if required). Return to the rinsed pan and bring to the boil, cooking for two minutes. Serve immediately with dice of fried bread handed separately; no other garnish is necessary.

# CARROT AND TARRAGON SOUP

*1½ lb carrots*
*2 medium onions*
*1 medium potato*
*1-2 pints stock – if making this soup for vegetarians use vegetable stock, otherwise use good chicken stock*
*2 teaspoons dried tarragon*
*1 oz butter*
*salt and pepper*

Melt butter and add roughly chopped vegetables, sweating onions for a few minutes first. Add stock, more may be required.
Bring to the boil, add tarragon and simmer gently for 45 minutes and make sure the carrots are cooked.
Liquidise and test for seasoning. Rinse out liquidiser jug with a little milk.
If necessary add a little more tarragon after liquidising.
Serve with a swirl of cream and a fresh tarragon leaf.

# MUSHROOM SOUP

*½ lb field mushrooms*
*1 shallot*
*1 pint milk and stock, or milk and water*
*1 oz butter*
*½ oz flour*
*2 egg yolks and ½ pint cream mixed (liaison)*
*salt and pepper*
*seasoning*
*bouquet garni*

Wipe mushrooms with a damp cloth and scrape the stalks. Reserve one or two for garnish.
Melt the fat and fry the shallot and mushrooms lightly.
Add the milk and stock, some seasoning and the bouquet garni.
Place lid on saucepan and cook until mushrooms are tender, about 20 minutes, then liquidise.
Place the flour in the rinsed saucepan and beat in the soup smoothly and gradually, stir until boiling. Strain in the liaison but do not allow to boil once this has been added. Add the mushroom garnish chopped small and when serving add some finely chopped parsley.

# SPRING SOUP

*large garden lettuce*
*12-15 spring onions*
*1 pint milk*
*1 pint stock*
*watercress*
*1 tablespoon cornflour*
*chopped parsley*
*salt and pepper*
*nutmeg*
*touch of sugar*

Wash lettuce and shred. Chop onions. Melt some dripping in saucepan and fry lettuce and onions for 5 minutes. Add stock and simmer for 10 minutes.

Mix cornflour with a little milk and pour into soup, stir until it boils, allow to simmer for another 10 minutes.

Add watercress for the last 2 minutes. Season to taste with salt, pepper, a little sugar and nutmeg. Liquidise and pass though sieve, cleaning out liquidiser with remaining milk.

Serve with chopped parsley or for a change with chopped watercress.

## BUTTER BEAN BROTH

*8 oz butter beans*
*4 oz streaky bacon*
*1 oz butter*
*onion*
*leek*
*celery*
*½ pint milk*
*2 tablespoons oil*
*large clove garlic*
*bay leaf*
*salt and pepper*

Cover butter beans with water and bring to the boil and boil for 1 minute. Leave to stand for 1 hour. Add bay leaf and rind and simmer for 45 minutes. Remove bay leaf and rind. Chop vegetables and sweat with the bacon in the oil for 10 minutes. Add the beans plus the cooking liquor. Cover and simmer for 20 minutes. Mash against side of pan but leave a few butter beans whole. Add milk to thin and serve piping hot. You can use a tin of butter beans in which case leave out the first step. Season to taste.

# FARMHOUSE TERRINE

6 oz chicken liver
6 oz minced belly pork
3 oz minced raw ham
8 oz streaky bacon
1 oz butter
small onion
1 clove of garlic
1 fl oz brandy
1 glass red wine
1 bay leaf
½ teaspoonful mixed herbs
1 small egg
salt and pepper
10 crushed juniper berries

Melt butter and fry onion, garlic and herbs over a fierce heat. Add the brandy and set alight. Add red wine and stir.
Add the rest of the ingredients (but not the cream and egg). Cook gently for a few minutes. Take off the heat and stir in the egg and cream (beaten together). Season.
Line paté tin with bacon, add the ingredients to tin. Cover tightly and place in a roasting tin half filled with water. Bake in a slow oven, Gas 3/325°F/160°C for 1¼ hours.
(Place in refrigerator when almost cool with heavy weights on top).

# PORK AND LIVER PATÉ

1 lb pig's liver
5 oz fat belly pork
3 rashers bacon
1 large or 2 small cloves garlic
2 fl oz white wine
salt and about 15 twists of black peppermill

Mince liver and pork, add seasoning, crushed garlic, chopped bacon and wine. Allow to stand in a bowl (not metal) for at least 2 hours in the fridge. Pack into a loaf tin (or a suitable terrine), cover and bake for 1 hour in a moderate oven. Remove cover and bake for a further 10 minutes.
(Some people like to stand the tin in a dish with water but this is not absolutely necessary).

## ROSEDEN LIVER PATÉ

*4 oz butter*
*8 oz lamb's liver (or chicken)*
*4 bacon rashers*
*1 small onion*
*4 oz mushrooms*
*¼ pint cream*
*a splash of best sherry*
*clove of garlic*

Melt butter, add onion (finely chopped), bacon rashers, garlic and liver. Slice mushrooms and add.
When cooked add sherry and cream.
Allow to cool and put through liquidiser or food processor. (Adjust seasoning).

# SALMON MOULD

*8 oz tinned or cooked salmon*
*1 packet gelatine*
*2 tablespoons wine vinegar*
*¼ small cucumber, finely chopped*
*½ onion, finely chopped*
*2 dessertspoons mayonnaise*
*salt and freshly ground black pepper*


Dissolve gelatine (according to instructions on packet) in wine vinegar and 1 tablespoon of juice from the salmon. Flake the salmon. Add all the other ingredients and pour into a salmon mould or ramekin dishes. Refrigerate until required.


# TUNA FISH MOUSSE

*2 oz butter*
*2 oz plain flour*
*½ pint milk*
*salt and pepper*
*1 tablespoon powdered gelatine*
*1 tablespoon water*
*2 x 7 oz tins tuna*
*¼ pint home-made mayonnaise*
*lemon juice*
*½ pint double cream*


Make white sauce with butter, flour and milk. Season.
Melt gelatine in water and add to sauce, mix well and stand aside to cool.
Drain and flake the tuna fish and add to sauce with the mayonnaise and lemon juice.
Whip the cream (not too stiff) and fold into the mixture.

# PRAWNS IN ROSEDEN SAUCE

*8 oz cooked and shelled prawns*
*10-15 oz home-made mayonnaise*
*1 teaspoon tomato purée*
*1 teaspoon horseradish sauce*
*1 teaspoon lemon juice*
*a little sugar*
*dash of tabasco*
*dash of double cream*
*stick of celery, finely chopped*
*½ green pepper, finely chopped*
*small piece cucumber, finely chopped*
*½ crisp eating apple, finely chopped*
*paprika*

Mix mayonnaise with tomato purée, sugar, cream, horseradish, tabasco and lemon juice. Mix prawns and other ingredients into the mayonnaise mixture. Serve on a bed of lettuce with a twist of lemon and cucumber to garnish. Lightly dust with paprika.


# CHICKEN AND BACON SURPRISE

*2 small chicken breasts (if available use smoked chicken)*
*4 slices smoked streaky bacon*
*lettuce*
*watercress*
*1 lemon*
*parsley to garnish*

Cut each slice of bacon in half, stretch with the back of a knife and roll. Grill or fry chicken together with bacon rolls. Cut each breast in half. Slice in a fan shape on a bed of lettuce and garnish with the bacon rolls, watercress and a twist of lemon. Sprinkle with lemon zest and chopped parsley.
If you use a full chicken breast per person, this makes an ideal lunch-time snack.

# HAM, PRUNE AND ORANGE TWIST

Serves 4

*12 small slices of thinly sliced cooked ham*
*8 cooked stoned prunes*
*large carton cottage cheese*
*horseradish sauce*
*4 thin slices of orange*
*lettuce*
*parsley*

For each serving roll three slices of ham and serve on a bed of lettuce. Sieve the cottage cheese and mix with a little horseradish sauce. Pile cheese onto ham, twist the orange slice and place a prune on either side of the orange slice on top of the cheese. Add a sprig of parsley and serve.

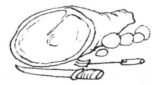

# AVOCADO WITH STILTON AND CREAM

*2 avocado pears, peeled*
*2 oz Stilton cheese*
*4 oz single cream*
*2 dessertspoons vegetable oil*
*juice of one small lemon*
*1 teaspoon Worcestershire sauce*
*grated onion (use a small onion)*
*chopped parsley*
*black pepper*

Beat the cheese and cream together until smooth. Add oil, lemon, Worcestershire sauce, onion and parsley. Season to taste.

Cut avocado pears in half and slice, fan shaped on to a bed of lettuce, putting a little of the Stilton mixture at the top with chopped walnuts on top of the cheese, serve with brown buttered bread triangles.

# TOMATO, AVOCADO AND MOZZARELLA ANTIPASTO

Serves 4
Suitable for vegetarians

*4 large ripe tomatoes*
*1 large ripe avocado, peeled*
*8 oz Mozzarella cheese*
*2 teaspoons red wine vinegar*
*½ teaspoon caster sugar*
*8 fresh basil leaves for garnish*

**Dressing**
*½ teaspoon salt*
*1 teaspoon dried oregano*
*2 tablespoons virgin olive oil*
*black pepper*

Wash, core and slice tomatoes and sprinkle with vinegar and sugar.

Slice cheese thinly. Halve avocado and slice flesh lengthwise. Arrange slices on plates, alternating colours.

Mix olive oil, black pepper, salt and oregano and sprinkle dressing evenly over each plate. Garnish with basil leaves.

# JOAN'S EGGY DISH

Use as a starter or a brunch dish

*4 eggs*
*1 large onion*
*8 button mushrooms*
*1 tablespoon tomato purée*
*4 – 6 oz grated cooking cheese*

**Sauce**
*¾ oz butter*
*¾ oz flour*
*½ pint milk*
*seasoning to taste*

Hard boil eggs.
Fry sliced onions and mushrooms.
Add tomato purée to pan together with seasoning.
Halve the eggs lengthways and arrange in an oval ovenproof dish.
Add the cooked onions and mushroom mixture.
Make a white sauce, adding the cheese, retain sufficient cheese to sprinkle on top after putting sauce over the eggs.
Brown in the oven for 10 minutes before serving.

**Handy hint**
*Rhubarb cooked in a stained saucepan will remove stain but don't eat the rhubarb afterwards!*

*A teaspoon of cream of tartar in a pint of water put into a stained aluminium pan and brought to the boil should get rid of the stain.*

# Main Meals

# GRANNY WALTON'S BEEF OLIVES

*6 slices braising steak (thinly sliced)*
*chopped onions*
*butter for frying*

**Stuffing**
*6 oz white bread crumbs*
*3 oz suet*
*mixed herbs (to taste)*
*salt and pepper*
*beaten egg*

Mix stuffing ingredients together using beaten egg to bind.
Fill each slice with the stuffing and roll up. Either skewer or tie.
Put a little butter and some chopped onions into frying pan and add beef olives, fry gently to brown.
Make gravy with residue in pan using flour and stock.
Put olives into casserole and add gravy.
Cook for approximately 1 hour in a moderate oven Gas 4/350°F/180°C.

# GREEK SHEPHERD'S PIE

*1lb steak mince*
*1 oz plain flour*
*½ pint Greek yoghurt*
*2 eggs – beaten*
*3 oz Cheddar cheese – grated*
*salt and pepper*

Whisk flour and yoghurt, add eggs, cheese, salt and pepper. Pour over cooked mince and cook for further 45 minutes until fluffy and golden brown. Oven Gas 4/350°F/180°C.

**Handy hint**
*Use a rolling pin to get the most out of a tube of tomato paste – or cut off the top.*

# MARY'S MEAT LOAF

*¾ lb mince*
*½ lb bacon – minced or cut fine*
*½ lb fresh white breadcrumbs*
*¼ pint milk*
*2 eggs*
*1 oz brown sugar*
*1 teaspoon dry mustard*
*salt and pepper*

Mix mince and bacon. Soak breadcrumbs in milk. Beat eggs with mustard. Mix all together and season well. Grease a loaf tin and sprinkle the brown sugar in the base. Press mixture into the tin. Cover with a loose wrapping of foil and bake for 1½ hours Gas 2/300°F/200°C.

# SHEPHERD'S PIE

*1 lb minced lamb or beef*
*carrot*
*onion*
*½ pint water or stock*
*2 lb potatoes*
*½ oz butter*
*1 tablespoon chopped chives*
*chopped parsley*
*nutmeg or mace*
*clove of garlic*

Finely chop carrot and onion and cook with mince in pan. Add parsley, nutmeg or mace and garlic (optional). For a change you can add tomato purée or a small tin of tomatoes. Thicken with a tablespoon of flour before adding the stock. Simmer ¾ hour. Meanwhile peel and cook potatoes. Cream with butter and warm milk. Add chopped chives tossed in a little butter over a gentle heat. Put mince into an ovenproof dish and fork over the potatoes. Cook in a fairly hot oven until the potatoes are nicely browned.

# BEEF BRAISED IN RED WINE WITH ONIONS AND MUSHROOMS

*2 lb of beef cut into slices approximately 1/4 in thick and 3 in long*
*3 tablespoons oil*
*2 medium sized carrots*
*2 large onions*
*2 cloves of garlic (crushed)*
*2 sprigs of thyme*
*1 bayleaf*
*6 – 8 rashers streaky bacon*
*salt and pepper*
*20 or more button onions*
*8 oz mushrooms*
*1 tablespoon flour*
*10 fl oz red wine*
*5 fl oz water*

Brown meat in oil in pan, set aside. Add sliced onion to pan, cook until transparent.
Add carrot. Return meat to pan. Sprinkle in 1 heaped tablespoon flour. Stir and gradually add red wine and water.
Add garlic, thyme, and bayleaf. Season with salt and pepper – not too much at this stage.
Cook for 2 hours in a slow oven. Gas 1/275°F/140°C.
Fry cubes of bacon and button onions, add and cook for a further ¾ to 1 hour.
Add mushrooms about 15 minutes before serving.

# STEAK AND KIDNEY PUDDING

*1-1½ lb stewing steak*
*2-3 lamb's kidneys*
*seasoning*
*a little flour*
*stock or water plus stock cube*

**Suet Crust**
*8 oz self-raising flour*
*pinch salt*
*4 oz suet*
*water to mix*

Trim meat and cut into cubes. Remove core from kidneys and chop into small pieces. Mix together and season well.

Sift together the flour and salt into mixing bowl. Add suet and enough water to mix to a firm dough. Turn on to a floured board and set aside one third for top of pudding. Roll remainder to a circle about ¼ inch thick. Line the inside of greased 2 pint pudding basin, fitting in the pastry gently.

Fill with meat mixture, sprinkling each layer with a little flour.

Add enough stock nearly to fill. Roll out reserved pastry to form a lid and cover pudding. Seal pastry edges and trim.

Cover with a double thickness of greased greaseproof paper or kitchen foil and steam for four hours.

Serve with thickened gravy.

# MOCK GAME

*1 lb beefsteak*
*2 or 3 rashers bacon*
*1 onion*
*1 oz butter*
*1 oz flour*
*½ pint stock*
*1 wine glass of vinegar*
*1 teaspoon redcurrant jelly*
*1 teaspoon capers*
*½ teaspoon lemon zest*
*salt and pepper*

Cut the meat into thin squares, lay a piece of bacon on each. Roll up and secure with thread or cocktail stick.

Dip in seasoned flour and fry in the butter. Take out the meat and brown the remainder of the flour. Add the stock, stirring until it boils.

Put in the meat, chopped onion, capers, lemon zest and vinegar and stew until tender. Arrange the meat on a hot dish and add the jelly to the gravy, season to taste. Strain gravy over the meat and garnish with sippets of fried bread.

# STEWED OX KIDNEY

*½ lb kidney*
*1 oz butter or dripping*
*1 oz flour*
*½ pint stock*
*1 small onion*
*1 teaspoon ketchup*
*1 teaspoon Worcestershire sauce*
*salt and pepper*

Scald the kidney and cut in neat slices, melt butter, fry onion and kidney. Brown the flour carefully, add stock, stir till it boils. Replace onion and kidney, add flavourings and seasoning. Simmer gently 2 hours, DO NOT BOIL. Serve with a border of boiled rice.

# STUFFED SHOULDER OF LAMB

Ask your family butcher to bone a shoulder of lamb but not to roll.
Make the following stuffing:
Fry 2 large onions until transparent, add herbs (to taste), salt and pepper, 8 oz breadcrumbs and bind with a beaten egg.
Trim any excess fat from lamb.
Put stuffing on the inside and roll up, tying firmly and cook as for roast lamb.

# NOISETTES OF LAMB

*1 loin of lamb, boned (for a more economical dish, best end can be used)*
*take the leaves from 4 good sprigs of mint and chop with parsley and fresh herbs,*
*preferably marjoram*
*a little salt and pepper*
*crushed garlic (optional)*

Sprinkle herbs over the inside of the boned loin, roll up and tie at 1½ inch intervals with thin twine. Cut off 8 noisettes.
Brush the noisettes with melted butter and place under the grill, turning once, for 8–10 minutes depending on thickness.

# SUMMER STEW

*2 lb neck of lamb*
*6 new potatoes*
*6 new carrots*
*6 new turnips*
*spring onions*
*peas*
*water or stock*
*salt and pepper*

Cut lamb into neat chops put in stewpan with enough water or stock to cover and bring to the boil. Remove scum.
Carefully prepare vegetables which should be small and equal in size. Put in pan, whole if possible, season. Simmer gently until cooked.
Add peas 15 minutes before ready. Adjust seasoning.

# PORK CHOPS WITH ORANGE

*4 pork chops*
*zest of one orange and juice*
*2 medium onions*
*chicken stock*
*plain flour*
*salt and pepper*

Fry chops until brown on both sides and soften onions. Take out of pan. Add flour to pan juices and cook for a minute. Add stock, zest and juice of orange.
Return chops to pan. Season. Simmer until chops are tender.

### Freezer tips
*Before putting a quiche in the freezer and before adding the filling brush base with margarine (melted) then add filling and freeze.*

*Always use a little bicarbonate of soda in the water when washing out the refrigerator or freezer.*

# PORK CHOPS IN WHITE WINE

*4 pork chops*
*2 medium onions, sliced*
*6 oz mushrooms, sliced*
*1 teaspoon dry mustard*
*10 fl oz (approximately) white wine*


Brown chops in butter, put into casserole. Set aside and fry onions and mushrooms.

Put onions, mushrooms and mustard in casserole with chops. Add white wine to frying pan to add to the juices.

Pour over chops, cover and cook for 1½ hours in a moderate oven, Gas 4/350°F/180°C. Garnish with watercress.


# CASSEROLED WOOD PIGEONS

*2 wood pigeons*
*seasoned flour*
*3 slices very fat bacon*
*2 large onions*
*8 large leaves of sage or 2 teaspoons dried sage*
*stock*
*flour to thicken*


Make sure pigeons are thoroughly clean, cut them in half lengthways and cover with seasoned flour. Dice bacon and put in frying pan to extract fat. Take out and put in casserole dish.

Put onions into fat in frying pan together with sage, fry until tender and add to bacon. Add more fat to frying pan if necessary, brown the birds all over. Lay the pigeons on the onions.

Add stock to frying pan and with a wooden spoon scrape the goodness in the pan into the stock. Add this to the casserole, covering the pigeons.

Cover the casserole and allow to simmer until birds are tender, about 1-1½ hours. Gas 4/350°F/180°C.

Adjust seasoning and thicken as necessary.

# CORONATION CHICKEN

*1 cooked chicken*
*grapes*
*mayonnaise*
*curry powder*
*apricots or apricot jam*
*Lee and Perrins Worcestershire Sauce*
*chutney*
*seasoning*

Mix mayonnaise to taste with other sauce ingredients. Add pieces of chicken to mixture. Decorate with grapes and serve.


# CHICKEN 'N' CHIPS

Serves 5-6

*2 cups cubed cooked chicken (or turkey)*
*½ cup slivered blanched toasted almonds*
*½ cup grated cheese*
*2 cups diced celery*
*2 tablespoons lemon juice*
*1 cup crushed potato crisps (salted)*
*2 tablespoons grated onion*
*½ teaspoon salt*
*1 cup mayonnaise*

Combine all ingredients except cheese and potato chips.
Pat lightly into an 8 inch × 8 inch × 1½ inch baking dish.
Sprinkle with grated cheese then with crushed potato crisps.
Bake in hot oven Gas 7/425°F/220°C for 15 – 20 minutes.
Serve warm rather than hot with a tossed salad.

# CHICKEN AND LEMON

*1 x 3½ lb chicken or chicken breast fillets*
*zest of a lemon and juice for the sauce*
*butter*
*salt and pepper*


Mix half of the zest, a little salt and pepper with sufficient butter to put over the chicken.
Put a little water in the roasting tin, add the chicken and cover with foil.
Cook for about one hour, Gas 4/350°F/180°C. Take off cover to brown. When the chicken is cooked, keep warm.
Drain off fat in tin. Reduce juices, add remaining lemon zest and juice. Thicken with a flour and butter paste or for a special occasion use double cream, but do not boil.
Decorate with lemon and a few toasted almonds.


# CHICKEN CASSEROLE

*1 chicken*
*1½ oz butter*
*4 oz ham or bacon cut small*
*1 carrot – sliced*
*2 or 3 spring onions*
*a few peppercorns*
*bunch of herbs*
*½ gill Marsala*
*1 gill chicken stock*


Joint the fowl neatly. Melt butter in a stew pan and add chicken pieces, bacon or ham, carrot and onions. Fry together until the chicken is nicely browned all over. Pour off all the fat, add Marsala and stock and the herbs and peppercorns. Cover and simmer gently in the oven for 1½ – 2 hours. Remove all fat from the gravy, add another gill of stock, and, if liked, another tablespoon of Marsala.

# CREAMED SWEETBREADS

*sweetbreads*
*white stock*
*2-3 egg yolks*
*cream*
*chopped parsley*
*salt, pepper and nutmeg*
*streaky bacon*

Blanch the sweetbreads in boiling water then put them in cold water. When quite cold, dry them and stew gently for half an hour in the stock. Beat the eggs with the cream, parsley and seasoning, add the stock the sweetbreads were cooked in and gently heat. Make bacon rolls by rolling up small slices of bacon and frying. Put the sweetbreads into an entrée dish, pour over the sauce and garnish with the bacon rolls.

# LIVER, ONION AND STREAKY BACON

*1½ lb lamb's liver*
*4 rashers streaky bacon*
*2 medium onions*
*oil or butter for frying*

Fry onions until transparent. Fry bacon.
Add liver and cook for approximately 3 minutes each side. Place in casserole and make gravy with residue in pan.
Pour over liver, bacon and onions. Cook in moderate oven for about 30 minutes.

# FARMHOUSE PIE

*12 oz beef mince*
*12 oz sausage meat*
*1 large onion*
*8 oz carrots – grated*
*7½ oz tomatoes*
*herbs*
*¼ pint water/beef stock*

***Suet crust***
*4 oz breadcrumbs*
*8 oz self-raising flour*
*5 oz suet*
*1 teaspoon salt*

Line pie dish with pastry – reserving sufficient for top.
Cook beef mince, sausagemeat and onion in a frying pan. Add herbs, stock and tomatoes, take off heat and add carrots.
Put mixture in pie dish and cover with remaining suet crust.
Bake in a fairly hot oven, Gas 5/375°F/190°C, until golden brown.

# JEAN'S PORK PIE

***Hot water crust pastry***
*1 lb plain flour*
*4 oz lard*
*1 teaspoon salt*
*¼ pint of water*

***Filling***
*lean cooked pork*
*gravy*

Sieve flour and salt. Melt lard in water and bring it to the boil.
Add to flour in a warm mixing bowl. Beat until a firm, smooth paste is formed.
Allow to cool slightly.
Roll out enough to line case (or cases) plus tops.
Fill with cooked lean pork, add 3 tablespoons of gravy. Seal top with beaten egg and make a hole in the centre. Decorate with pastry leaves. Brush over with beaten egg.
Cook at Gas 6/400°F/200°C for 1 hour or 40-50 minutes for small pies.
Allow pie to cool, pour in enough warm stock to fill up pie. Leave until cold.
If you think stock is not thick enough add a little gelatine.

# ANNE'S GAME PIE

*Pastry as before*

Line tin with pastry and put in approximately 3 oz each – cooked sausage meat and chopped bacon. Layer with cranberry jelly, add diced game (whatever may be available and/or to taste) and continue layers until full. Add top as for pork pie. If a large pie make one or two holes. Glaze top. Cook Gas 6/400°F/200°C for 1 hour.
Add one teaspoonful of Agar Agar to the stock from the game – or, if preferred use gelatine. Add the stock as for pork pie.

# HAM AND EGG PIE

*12 oz lean ham*
*4 eggs*
*milk*
*seasoning*

**Shortcrust pastry**
*8 oz plain flour*
*4 oz hard margarine*
*1 oz lard*
*salt*
*cold water*

Cut margarine and lard into pieces and add to sieved flour and salt. Mix to breadcrumb consistency and add sufficient water to make a soft and pliable dough.
Line an 8 inch pie dish, retaining sufficient pastry for the top.
Fry ham, cut into small pieces. Whisk eggs with a little milk.
Place ham in pastry base and add seasoned egg and milk (taking care not to over salt if ham is at all salty).
Place lid on top and glaze.
Cook centre of the oven for approximately 25-30 minutes at Gas 4-6/350°F-400°F/180°C-200°C.

# NUTTY FRUIT RISOTTO

For the vegetarian

*12 oz easy cook brown rice*
*9 oz packet ready-to-eat dried fruit salad*
*3 celery sticks*
*1 large onion*
*2 tablespoons groundnut or sunflower oil*
*½ oz butter or sunflower margarine*
*½ teaspoon ground cinnamon*
*½ teaspoon ground ginger*
*salt and freshly ground black pepper*
*1-2 tablespoons fresh coriander*
*3½ oz mix of sunflower seeds and nuts.*

Roughly chop fruit salad, trim and chop celery sticks, peel and finely chop onion.

Heat oil and butter in large pan until butter melts. Add onion and celery and cook over a gentle heat, stirring frequently for 8 minutes until vegetables are soft and golden.

Add chopped fruit and 1½ pints of water, bring to the boil, cover and simmer for ten minutes.

Add rice, ground cinnamon and ginger, season to taste with salt and freshly milled pepper. Stir thoroughly.

Cover and cook over moderate heat until rice is cooked and all the liquid is absorbed.

Fold in sunflower seeds and nuts and half the coriander, check seasoning. Sprinkle in remaining coriander.

# VEGETABLE ROLY-POLY

*3 carrots*
*3 parsnips*
*1 small turnip*
*3 potatoes (sliced)*
*3 tomatoes*
*salt and pepper to taste*
*a little gravy powder*
*suet crust (see steak and kidney pudding recipe but use vegetarian suet if for vegetarians)*

Roll out the suet crust fairly thinly, sprinkle over with gravy powder.
Over the crust lay the grated carrots, parsnips, turnip and sliced potatoes.
Cover with a layer of sliced tomatoes. Season.
Roll up in a cloth and steam for 2½ hours. Serve steaming hot with a little
good gravy.

**Handy hint**
*Rub a burn mark (caused by a spark from the fire) with the edge of a 10p coin.*

**Handy hint**
*Before using rubber gloves, turn inside out and put a piece of sticking plaster across
the top of each finger to avoid long nails cutting into them too quickly.*

### Handy hint
*When cleaning silver – particularly inside teapots, coffee pots, jugs, etc use washing soda and silver tops from milk bottles.*

### A Polishing Cloth
*Make your own polishing cloths.*
*Dissolve ½lb of soap (shred it first) in ½ pint of boiling water add 4 oz whitening and a tablespoon of ammonia. When cool beat to a jelly. Put in some squares of cotton (soft linen if available) or smooth dusters and soak for 12 hours. Squeeze out and leave to dry. Good for any polishing, especially silver and metal.*

### Spring Cleaning
*Use a matt oil-based paint rather than emulsion to cover a water stain on a ceiling.*
*Paint brushes that need cleaning – use a well known brand of paint stripper.*
*Put a little detergent into warm water when damping and stripping old wallpaper.*
*Always store paint tins, with lid firmly on, upside down when painting is finished.*
*Run out of rawlplugs – for a makeshift use an old spent match.*
*Use lemon juice to get rid of a green stain in the bath.*

### To revive furniture
*Use equal parts of linseed oil, vinegar and turpentine (add 2 teaspoons of sugar to each pint – optional). Shake well. Cleans as well as polishes.*

### A Sweet Sachet Filling
*Take equal quantities of lavender flowers, dried rosemary, pounded orris-root, dried rose petals (tea roses or the old fashioned cabbage roses are the sweetest), and a few leaves of scented verbena or sweet geranium. Crush all together into a coarse powder. Put into muslin bags.*

# Savouries and Vegetable Dishes

# SMOKED SALMON QUICHE

*8 oz smoked salmon pieces*
*4 slices bacon and 1 medium onion chopped – cooked together in 1 oz butter*
*2 large eggs*
*½ pint single cream*
*pinch of mixed herbs or if available fresh fennel*
*salt and pepper*


Prepare a flan case (using 6 oz of short crust pastry). If wished this can be cooked blind but this is not really necessary.

After thoroughly cooking the onion and bacon add salt and pepper and herbs (a word of caution, make sure the bacon is not too salty before adding the extra salt).

Whisk together the eggs and cream. Add the cooled bacon and onion and smoked salmon. Put in flan case.

(If preferred – an added extravagance – use slices of smoked salmon and try to layer with the mixture).

Place in the centre of the oven and cook for about 30 minutes until the quiche is golden brown, Gas 5/375°F/190°C.


# CHEESE AND ONION QUICHE

Suitable for vegetarians

*Flan case as before – again no need to bake blind.*
*12 oz cooking cheese – preferably Cheddar (red)*
*2 good sized onions*
*2 large eggs*
*½ pint cream*
*salt and pepper*
*mixed herbs*


Grate cheese putting a little on the base of the flan.

Fry onion and add to beaten eggs and cream with salt and pepper and a good sprinkling of mixed herbs.

Add most of the cheese, reserving a little to sprinkle on the top of the flan.

Pour into flan case and cook as above. Gas 5/325°F/190°C.
Cook for 5 minutes at a slightly hotter temperature at the top of the oven and then move to centre for the rest of the time – this helps to set the custard mixture.
(If wished add sliced tomatoes to the top about half way through the cooking).

# ONIONS ON TOAST

A nice change to Welsh Rarebit

*onions*
*cheese*
*hot buttered toast*
*mustard*
*salt and pepper*

Fry sliced onions until golden brown and spread thickly over hot buttered toast. Season.
Cover with thin slices of cheese and a little mustard.
Grill. If you are lucky enough to have an Aga or Rayburn pop in the hot oven.
Serve as soon as the cheese has melted.

# FRENCH BEAN OMELETTE

*2 tablespoons French beans*
*4 eggs*
*2 tablespoons Parmesan cheese*
*pepper and salt*

Cut up finely 2 tablespoons of French beans, stir into them 4 well-beaten eggs, add 2 tablespoonfuls of grated Parmesan cheese, pepper and salt to taste. When perfectly mixed put the whole with 2 oz melted butter into an omelette pan and fry approximately 3 minutes.

# A QUICK VEGETARIAN DISH

*3 oz macaroni*
*2 oz finely grated cheese*
*1 oz butter*
*black pepper and salt*

Boil macaroni for nearly 30 minutes and drain. Return to the same pan, stir into it finely grated cheese and butter. The cheese should be stirred in half at a time and well shaken among the macaroni. Season with black pepper and salt and serve. (This was a recipe before the days of tinned macaroni cheese).

# GRETA'S POTATO CONCOCTION

*potatoes*
*onions*
*milk*
*butter*
*salt and pepper*

Peel potatoes and slice into ⅛ inch slices. Slice onions to the same thickness. Layer potatoes and onions into an ovenproof dish until filled, seasoning each layer with salt and pepper.
Dot with butter and three-quarter fill with milk. Bake in a moderate oven until cooked.
Add garlic and/or herbs to vary the dish.

# CREAMED POTATOES WITH CHIVES

Boil potatoes, rice or mash (near the door to make them fluffy). Heat some creamy milk with half a cupful of finely chopped chives. As soon as the milk boils add to the potatoes.

# AN ONION CAKE

*sliced potatoes*
*butter*
*finely chopped onion*
*salt and pepper*

Butter an ovenproof oval or round dish.
Lay some sliced potatoes in the bottom of the dish.
Cover with onions and some tiny bits of butter.
Sprinkle with salt and pepper.
Repeat until dish is full, finishing with a layer of potatoes, dot with butter and cover with buttered piece of foil.
Bake for approximately 1 hour in a moderate oven. Gas 4/350°F/180°C.
Remove foil 5 minutes before serving to brown potatoes.

# CRISPY ONIONS

*8-12 small onions*
*2 tablespoons flour*
*1 cupful of breadcrumbs*
*½ pint milk*
*½ pint water*
*3 oz margarine*
*cayenne pepper*

Peel onions and boil them in the milk and water.
When tender, remove from pan, do not break them.
Grease a roasting tin or pie dish and put in onions.
Make the sauce with the liquid from the onions. Season to taste.
Pour over the onions. Bind the breadcrumbs with just enough melted margarine to make a firm mixture. Spread over sauce.
Bake in a hot oven until golden brown.

**Handy hint**
*Equal quantities of water and vinegar left overnight in a kettle will de-scale it. Rinse thoroughly next morning.*

# LEEKS WITH BACON ROLLS

*leeks*
*milk*
*streaky bacon*

Blanch leeks in boiling water and then cook slowly in milk.
Drain when cooked, keep warm. Make a sauce with the milk, (add a butter
and flour liaison and cook, stirring all the time) season to taste.
Add a touch of cream to the sauce, if liked.
Grill tiny rolls of streaky bacon until crisp. Pour sauce over leeks and top with
the bacon rolls.


# CREAMED CELERY

*large head of celery*
*1 pint milk*
*1 oz butter*
*1 oz flour*
*4 oz grated cooking cheese*
*breadcrumbs fried in butter until golden*
*salt and pepper*

Wash celery thoroughly. Cut into 2 inch strips or dice.
Put in a pan with milk and salt. Cook until tender.
Drain off milk – make sauce with this.
Let the sauce boil for a few minutes before adding cheese and seasoning as
required. Add the celery.
Put in dish and sprinkle with breadcrumbs.


# COLESLAW IN LIME JELLY

*1 lime jelly*
*½ teaspoon salt*
*1 tablespoon finely grated onion*
*grated cabbage*
*1 carrot, grated*
*small green pepper, grated*

Make jelly with just over 12 fluid ounces of water and add 1 tablespoon white vinegar (or brown if white not available). Allow the jelly to set slightly, then add 1 cup grated cabbage, 1 grated carrot, a little grated green pepper and a few chopped olives (optional). Turn into mould and allow to set.

# POTATO PANCAKES

*2 large potatoes*
*2 medium onions*
*2 tablespoons flour*
*2 eggs*
*little salt and pepper (I sometimes use celery salt for flavour)*

Grate potatoes and onions into a basin, add flour and seasoning. Mix with eggs into a slightly soft paste.
Put butter and olive oil into frying pan. Drop a tablespoonful of mixture into the pan. Turn when brown underneath.
Keep warm while cooking remaining pancakes.

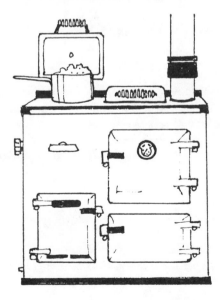

# CHEESE SPREAD

*2 eggs – beaten*
*1 lb Cheddar cheese – grated*
*1 teaspoon mustard powder*
*½ pint milk*
*1 oz butter or margarine*
*salt and pepper*


Beat eggs in a pan. Stir in the cheese, mustard and milk. Add butter and stir over a moderate heat until it begins to thicken. Cool and store in the fridge in a covered container. This keeps for up to a month. Use to make cheese on toast – spread thickly and grill, sandwiches, or stir into hot pasta. Thin with milk to make a cheese sauce.


**Handy hint**
*A little lemon juice mixed with a brass cleaner will keep brass clean a little longer.*

**Hot Treacle Possett for a sniffly cold**
*Put a pint of milk into a pan and bring almost to the boil. Add 2 tablespoons of treacle and the juice of a lemon and boil carefully until the curd separates. Strain and drink hot.*

**Elderflower Ointment**
*1 lb clarified lard*
*1 gallon of elderflower heads*
*Melt the lard, add the elderflowers and boil until a pulp.*
*Strain through a fine sieve and add a few drops of turpentine.*
*Put into small jars and allow to set.*
*Good for healing bruises, sores, rough hands, heat lumps and bites.*
*Without turpentine and with a few drops of oil of lavender can be used as a face cream.*

**Handy hint**
*Cotton wool buds are very useful in the kitchen, cleaning narrow spouts, behind the taps, in small crevices.*

*For greasy marks on wallpaper use a warm iron on some blotting paper. (Hope you have some! Blotting paper, I mean.)*

# Desserts

# LEMON CHEESECAKE

*6 oz digestive biscuits*
*2 oz margarine*
*3 dessertspoons syrup*
*1 oz sugar*
*1 large tin Nestlés condensed milk*
*7 oz Philadelphia cream cheese*
*2 lemons*

Crush biscuits and mix with melted margarine and syrup and sugar. Press into a flan dish or tin. Grate rind and squeeze juice from lemons. Whizz cheese, condensed milk and juice and rind in a food processor. Pour onto base and chill until set. Decorate top to suit.

# ORANGE FLUFF

*tin of mandarin oranges*
*1 packet of gelatine*
*8 oz sugar*
*1 orange, juice and zest*
*2 egg whites*

Use the juice of the orange and the juice from the tin and sprinkle over the gelatine, leave for five minutes and then put in warm place for a further five minutes to allow to dissolve (put over a pan of warm water if necessary). Add the zest from the orange.
Arrange mandarin oranges in bottom of souffle dish.
Put everything into a bowl and whisk. Pour over oranges and refrigerate until set.

# LEMON ICE CREAM

*4 large lemons*
*2 tablespoons sugar*
*6 eggs*
*1 large tin condensed milk*
*1 pint of double cream*

Mix egg yolks, sugar, milk, juice and rinds of lemons.
Whip cream. Whip egg whites. Mix all together and freeze in containers.

# CHOCOLATE CREAM

Whip 1 pint of double cream.
Grate ¾ lb dark chocolate and mix with 2 tablespoons brandy and 2 tablespoons demerara sugar.
Layer cream and chocolate mixture alternately in a dish or individual glasses.

# LEMON MERINGUE PIE

*6 oz shortcrust pastry*
*2 small lemons*
*½ pint milk*
*2 tablespoons sugar*
*2 eggs (separated)*
*1 heaped dessertspoon cornflour*

Line greased pie dish with pastry. Bake blind (circle of greaseproof in the bottom with rice or beans on top, remove when pastry set and brown a little further).
Blend cornflour with a little milk. Boil rest of milk and pour on to cornflour, return to pan. Add sugar, grated rind of lemons and juice with the beaten egg yolks. Stir until set.
Pour into cooked pastry case. Whisk egg whites with a little sugar and pile on top of pie.
Brown in a cool oven Gas 2/300°F/150°C.
Can be served cold or slightly warm.

# CHOUX PASTRY

For profiteroles – sweet or savoury

*2 oz butter*
*2 oz plain flour and pinch of salt sieved*
*2 standard eggs*
*¼ pint water*

Bring butter and water to boiling point in a saucepan. Remove from heat, add sieved flour and salt. Beat for a few minutes over very gentle heat with a wooden spoon until the paste forms a ball and the sides of the saucepan are clean.
Allow to cool slightly. Put in clean bowl of mixer and beat with the beater, slow speed at first while adding the eggs.
Turn to maximum speed for approximately 1 minute.
Put in forcing bag with plain nozzle. Pipe rounds and bake in hot oven Gas 6/400°F/200°C for about thirty minutes until well risen and crisp.
Make a small hole to allow steam to escape.

Use with savoury fillings or with cream inside with a chocolate sauce (as in eclairs) but pile together in a pyramid shape for a special sweet.


# HAZELNUT MERINGUE

*4 egg whites*
*3 oz toasted hazelnuts, fairly finely chopped*
*9 oz caster sugar*
*½ teaspoon cinnamon*

Line two 7-8 inch cake tins with baking parchment. Beat egg whites until stiff, add half the sugar and beat. Mix cinnamon with the remaining sugar and fold carefully into the egg whites. Fold in the nuts. Divide between the cake tins and bake in a cool oven (the simmering oven of an Aga cooker is ideal) Gas 1-2/275°F/140°C for about 1 hour. Turn out of tins and cool. Sandwich together with whipped cream.

# ROSEDEN SURPRISE

*½ pint cream*
*2 oranges*
*Cointreau or Grand Marnier*
*3 meringues – crushed, but not too small*

Grate the rind of the oranges and squeeze the juice. Whip cream until thick and fold in the rind, juice and liqueur. Fold in the crushed meringues. Freeze. Defrost for 15 minutes before serving in pretty glasses.

# RICH CHOCOLATE MOUSSE

This rich concoction will serve 6

*4 oz plain chocolate*
*3 oz unsalted butter*
*2 egg yolks*
*3 egg whites*
*2 tablespoons caster sugar*
*2 tablespoons flavouring – I use Grand Marnier*

Melt the chocolate in a large bowl and add the liqueur. Add the butter in small pieces and stir until all the butter is melted. Stir in the egg yolks. Whisk egg whites until stiff and slowly add the sugar while continuing to whisk until stiff and glossy. Fold gently into the chocolate mixture. Pour into one large bowl or individual bowls and refrigerate. Decorate the top with whipped cream or chocolate curls.

# CHOCOLATE MAPLE SYRUP PUDDING

*4 oz butter*
*4 oz caster sugar*
*3 oz self-raising flour*
*2 eggs*
*2 level tablespoons cocoa powder*
*1 tablespoon milk*
*pinch salt*
*vanilla essence*
*1 oz pecan nuts*

**Sauce**
*4 oz plain chocolate*
*¼ pint maple syrup*
*¼ pint hot water*

Grease a deep 7 inch cake tin. Melt chocolate in a bowl over a pan of simmering water. Mix the maple syrup with the hot water and stir into the melted chocolate. Meanwhile, sieve the flour, cocoa powder and salt into a bowl. Beat the butter and sugar until creamy. Add the eggs and continue to beat. Stir in the flour and cocoa, vanilla and chopped nuts. If you have a food processor you can put in everything except the nuts and process for a few seconds, add nuts and process for 1 or 2 seconds only. Spoon the mixture into the cake tin and carefully pour the sauce over the top. Bake at Gas 5/375°F/190°C for about 40 minutes. Turn out onto a large deepish dish. You can cook it in an Aga cooker on the grid shelf in the roasting oven with the plain baking sheet above it, but only for about 30 minutes.

# COFFEE BRANDY GATEAU

*12 trifle sponges*
*6 oz butter*
*6 oz caster sugar*
*3 large eggs*
*¼ pint double cream*
*1 tablespoon brandy*
*2 teaspoons coffee essence (or powdered coffee mixed with brandy)*
*chopped walnuts*

Line a soufflé dish with baking parchment. Cream butter and sugar until light and creamy. Beat in the eggs one at a time, then beat in the coffee and brandy. Cut the trifle sponges into three lengthwise and arrange a layer on the base of the souffle dish. Cover with some of the mixture. Arrange more sponges on the top and pour over the rest of the mixture. Finally cover with another layer of sponges. Press well down, put a saucer on top with a weight on that. Refrigerate for at least 3 hours. Shortly before serving, run the blade of a knife round the side of the dish and turn out. Decorate with whipped cream and walnuts.

## BRANDY BASKETS

*4 oz butter*
*3 oz caster sugar*
*3 oz plain flour*
*4 level tablespoons syrup*
*2 teaspoons ground ginger*
*1 teaspoon brandy*

Melt butter and sugar and syrup in a large saucepan. Add flour and ginger and brandy and mix well. Place teaspoons of the mixture well apart on greased baking sheets. Bake in a fairly hot oven Gas 6/400°F/200°C for 7-8 minutes (check after 5 minutes and watch carefully after that). Leave to cool slightly and shape over an orange or apple. Fill with whipped cream flavoured with crystallised ginger.

## FUDGY CREAM

*½ pint double cream*
*large carton natural yoghurt*
*muscovado sugar*

Whip cream until thick and fold in the yoghurt. Pour into one large dish or individual dishes and cover top with ½ inch sugar. Leave overnight. The sugar will dissolve through the cream and have a wonderful fudgy taste. Serve.

# FRUIT BRULÉE

*1 lb any fruit – fresh or tinned or frozen and defrosted*
*large carton low fat fromage frais*
*demerara sugar*

Put fruit into the bottom on an ovenproof dish and cover with fromage frais. Cover fromage frais with a thick layer of sugar – 3-4 tablespoons. Grill under a grill or in the top of a hot oven for about 5 minutes or until sugar bubbles. Chill and serve.

# PECAN PIE

**Pastry base**
*6 oz flour*
*3 oz butter and lard*
*water*

**Filling**
*3 eggs*
*8 oz soft dark brown sugar*
*3 oz melted butter*
*6 tablespoons dark syrup (half treacle, half syrup)*
*8 oz pecan nuts (shelled)*
*1 teaspoon vanilla essence*
*1 teaspoon salt*

Make pastry, line a flan dish and bake blind Gas 6/400°F/200°C.
Lightly beat the eggs and beat in the sugar, vanilla and salt. Stir in the melted butter, syrup and most of the pecans (chopped) – reserve a few to decorate the top. Pour into partially baked pastry case. Bake in the middle of the oven on a hot baking sheet for 35-40 minutes or until the filling is set. Gas 4/350°F/180°C.

# TREACLE SPONGE

*¼ pint syrup*
*4 oz flour*
*4 oz butter*
*4 oz caster sugar*
*2 eggs*
*2 tablespoons milk*
*½ teaspoon baking powder*
*vanilla essence*
*pinch salt*

Grease an ovenproof dish. Sieve together the flour, salt, baking powder. Cream butter and sugar and beat in the eggs one at a time. Fold in the flour and a few drops of vanilla essence. Cover bottom of dish with syrup, I always use more rather than less. Spoon in pudding mixture. Bake in a moderate oven Gas 4/350°F/180°C for about 30 minutes.

# GRANNY WALTON'S CHRISTMAS PUDDING

*½ lb suet*
*½ lb raisins*
*½ lb sultanas*
*½ lb currants*
*¼ lb breadcrumbs*
*¼ lb plain flour*
*2 oz mixed peel*
*1 oz almonds, coarsely chopped*
*½ teaspoon nutmeg*
*1 lemon*
*3 eggs*
*1 pint milk*

Mix ingredients well together and place in greased basins. Cover with greaseproof and tie cloths over the tops. Steam or boil for as long as you can but certainly for 6 or more hours. They can sit happily in pans with 2 or 3 inches of water in the simmering oven of an Aga cooker overnight but make sure there is enough water there before you go to bed! After the first boiling replace cloth covers and store. To serve, boil for a further 2-3 hours.

# RICH MOIST CHRISTMAS PUDDING

This recipe makes ten 2 pound puddings – useful as presents!

*1¼ lb plain flour*
*1 lb 14 oz brown sugar*
*1 lb 14 oz margarine*
*2 lb 8 oz fresh breadcrumbs*
*10 level tablespoons marmalade*
*10 lb dried fruit*
*20 eggs*
*2½ pints ale or stout*
*5 level teaspoons baking powder*
*5 level teaspoons ground nutmeg*
*2½ level teaspoons salt*
*2½ level teaspoons cinnamon*
*5 level teaspoons mixed spice*

Cream fat and sugar and add flour and spices and crumbs alternately with eggs. Add marmalade and finally the ale or stout, mixing well – don't forget to wish! Put into greased basins with greaseproof and cloth tops tied tightly round. Boil for 6 hours or more. To serve, boil for a further 2-3 hours.

# Cakes
# and Biscuits

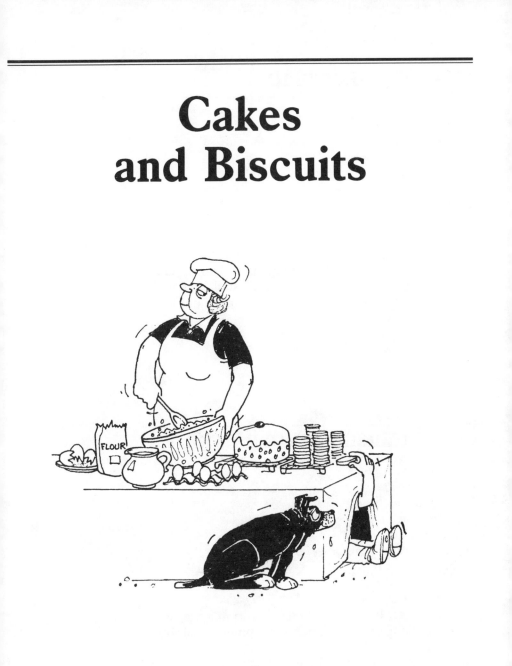

# ANN'S GINGERBREAD

*1 cup sugar*
*1 cup milk*
*4 oz margarine*
*8 oz self-raising flour*
*1 teaspoon ginger*
*1 teaspoon bicarb*
*2 tablespoons syrup*
*1 egg*

Put sugar, milk, margarine and syrup in pan to melt.
Dissolve bicarbonate of soda in a little milk and add flour and beaten egg.
Put in tin and bake in moderate oven for 1 hour at Gas 3/325°F/160°C.


# CRYSTALLISED GINGER CAKE

*3 oz butter*
*3 oz caster sugar*
*6 oz self-raising flour*
*1 dessertspoon golden syrup*
*2 oz crystallised ginger*
*½ teaspoon ground ginger (or to taste)*
*2 eggs*

Beat the sugar, butter and golden syrup to a cream.
Sieve the flour, ground ginger and a pinch of salt together. Add 1 egg and a little flour and beat well.
Add second egg and a little more flour and beat again.
Fold in remaining flour and a little milk if necessary.
Add the grated crystallised ginger and beat again.
Bake in a moderate oven for about 45 – 50 minutes. Gas 4/350°F/180°C.

# LEMON DRIZZLE

4 oz margarine or butter
6 oz caster sugar
6 oz self-raising flour
4 tablespoons milk
2 large eggs
juice and rind of 1 lemon

Mix all ingredients, except for lemon juice, together in bowl for 2 minutes.
Put into loaf tin and cook at Gas 3/325°F/160°C for 45-50 minutes.
When cooked pierce the top with a needle and pour over lemon juice mixed
with a little icing sugar.

# HEDGEHOG CAKE

From Australia

½ lb rich tea biscuits
4 oz margarine
6 oz icing sugar
1 egg
1 teaspoon vanilla essence or flavouring
1 level tablespoon drinking chocolate

Heat margarine, sugar and drinking chocolate in pan on gentle heat. Add
beaten egg; crush biscuits and add to mixture.
Mix well and press into baking tray.
Allow to cool and then cover with a chocolate icing.

*Handy hint*
*Without baking powder in the house? Use this recipe (providing you have these
ingredients!).*
*4 oz cream of tartar and 2 oz of bicarbonate of soda well mixed together.*

# CHOCOLATE CAKE

*4 oz margarine*
*4 oz sugar*
*1 dessertspoon syrup*
*vanilla essence*
*4 teaspoons milk*
*4 oz self-raising flour*
*1 tablespoon cocoa*
*2 eggs*

Mix fat and sugar to light and fluffy stage, add syrup. Add beaten eggs and milk. Sieve flour and cocoa together and fold into mixture. Add a little vanilla essence.
Put into 7-8 inch cake tin. Bake Gas 2/300°F/150°C for 20-25 minutes.

# ALL IN ONE CHOCOLATE CAKE

*6 oz self-raising flour*
*6 oz margarine*
*2 eggs*
*6 oz sugar*
*1 tablespoon cocoa dissolved in sufficient boiling water*

Beat all ingredients together for 2 minutes. Put in loaf tin and bake at Gas 4/350°F/180°C for 35-40 minutes.

# SANDWICH CAKE

(An older recipe than the present day all in one method but guaranteed to turn out well)

*2 oz margarine*
*2 eggs*
*4 oz sugar*
*4 oz flour*
*1 teaspoon baking powder*
*3 dessertspoons milk*

Beat margarine and sugar until white, add eggs one at a time and fold in sifted flour and baking powder.
Add the milk but do not allow to touch the bottom of the basin.
Bake for 20-25 minutes in a moderate oven.

# SWISS ROLL

*2½ oz sifted self-raising flour*
*3 eggs*
*4 oz caster sugar*

Heat oven to Gas 8/230°C/450°F. Bake sugar on a baking tray in the oven for 6 minutes.
Break eggs on to the sugar and beat until it trebles itself.
Add flour and pour into Swiss roll tin and bake for 6 minutes at the above temperature.
Turn on to sugared paper and spread with warmed raspberry jam and roll.
Will not crack when rolled.

# REALLY FRUITY CAKE

(Very moist)

*1 lb margarine*
*1 lb demerara sugar*
*1 lb 4 oz self-raising flour*
*2½ lb mixed fruit*
*4 eggs*

Melt margarine and sugar in pan. Stir in flour, fruit and eggs.
Put in Swiss roll tin and cook at Gas 3/325°F/160°C for 35-40 minutes. When cool cut into small squares.

# THE GAMEKEEPER'S WIFE'S FRUIT CAKE

*12 oz soft brown sugar*
*12 oz plain flour*
*12 oz margarine (use butter if keeping for any length of time)*
*1 level teaspoon baking powder*
*1 teaspoon freshly grated nutmeg*
*1 teaspoon mixed spice*
*½ teaspoon cinnamon*
*4 oz mixed peel*
*6 oz glacé cherries*
*12 oz currants*
*8 oz seedless raisins*
*12 oz sultanas*
*pinch of salt*
*6 eggs*
*4 tablespoons brandy or 2 tablespoons sherry*

Mix margarine or butter and sugar, add eggs and other ingredients. Bake for 4 hours at Gas 3/160°C/350°F.

# FARMHOUSE FRUIT CAKE

*8 oz margarine*
*8 oz caster sugar*
*4 eggs – beaten*
*8 oz plain flour*
*½ teaspoon mixed spice*
*8 oz raisins*
*8 oz currants and sultanas mixed*
*4 oz glacé cherries*

Cream together margarine and sugar until fluffy. Add eggs, a little at a time. Fold in flour and spice, sieved together. Fold in fruit.
Turn into prepared tin. Sprinkle halved cherries and flaked almonds on top. Bake at Gas 1-2/300°F/150°C.
Cook approximately 2-2½ hours.

# SLAB CAKE

½ lb sultanas
½ lb butter or margarine
½ lb sugar
½ lb currants
4 oz mixed peel
10 oz flour
2 teaspoons baking powder
3 eggs
a little milk to mix

Cream butter and sugar until light and fluffy. Add eggs beaten with a little milk alternately with flour.
Add fruit (sprinkled with a little flour) and add more milk if necessary.
Bake in a moderate oven for about 1 hour.

# ECONOMICAL BOILED FRUIT CAKE

2 cups of flour
1 cup of brown sugar
2 tablespoons lard
1 teaspoon mixed spice
1 teaspoon bicarbonate of soda mixed in boiling water
½ lb currants
½ lb raisins
lemon peel
pinch of salt

Boil the lard, sugar, fruit and spice together with one cup of boiling water for 5 minutes. When cool mix in the flour and soda. Put in a well-greased tin and bake for approximately 1 hour in a moderate oven. Gas 4/350°F/180°C.

***Handy hint***
*Baking powder, (slightly different)*
*½ lb ground rice*
*3 oz tartaric acid*
*4 oz bicarbonate of soda*

# JULIE'S CAKE

1 lb margarine
2 lb self-raising flour
12 oz sugar
4 tablespoons syrup or runny honey
4 cups dried fruit
4 teaspoons baking powder
4 eggs

**Icing**
icing sugar
lemon juice

Melt the sugar, margarine and syrup (or honey) in a pan. Cool. Mix in flour, baking powder, eggs and fruit. Put into Swiss roll tins and bake for 20-30 minutes Gas 2-3/300-325°F/150°-160°C. Coat with lemon icing while hot. Cut into squares when cold.

# DIANE'S FRUIT CAKE

1 lb margarine
1 lb demerara sugar
1 lb 4 oz self-raising flour
2½ lb mixed fruit
4 eggs

Melt margarine and sugar in a saucepan and cool. Stir in the remaining ingredients. Put into a Swiss roll tin and bake for 25-30 minutes Gas 3/325°F/160°C.

# ALMOND CAKE

*6 oz caster sugar*
*4 oz butter*
*2 eggs*
*2 drops almond essence*
*2 oz ground almonds*
*6 oz self-raising flour*
*2 dessertspoons milk*
*a little icing sugar*

Beat sugar and butter to light and fluffy stage.
Add beaten eggs alternately with flour and ground almonds (milk added to eggs), add almond essence.
Pour into 7½ inch cake tin. Cook for 1 hour at Gas 3/325°F/160°C. Dust with icing sugar when cool.

# ICED CRUNCH

*1 cup self-raising flour*
*½ cup sugar*
*1 cup coconut*
*2 cups cornflakes*
*4 oz melted butter*

Melt butter slowly. Add other ingredients and mix well together. Put into baking tray. Bake at Gas 5/375°F/190°C for 20 minutes.
Ice and allow to cool before cutting into squares.

# MUM'S SYRUP TART

**Pastry for base**
*6 oz self-raising flour*
*3 oz butter*
*2 fl oz milk*
*½ egg*
*pinch of salt*

**Pastry for top**
*4 oz butter*
*2 oz caster sugar*
*½ egg*
*6 oz flour*

**Filling**
*5 oz bread crumbs*
*16 fl oz syrup*

Make up both pastries and line dish.
Heat syrup and add bread crumbs, pour on to base.
Roll out top pastry and cut into strips and cover syrup with trellis pattern.
Cook 20 minutes at Gas 4/350°F/180°C.

# BUTTER TARTS

*shortcrust pastry to line shallow, rounded bun tins*
*1 egg*
*1 cup currants*
*1 cup brown sugar*
*butter (size of an egg)*
*pinch of salt*
*nutmeg*

Mix ingredients and put in to pastry shells and bake. This is a good substitute for mince pies.

**Handy hint**
*Place your candles in the deep freeze for one or two hours before using – they will burn longer.*

# BORDER TART

*Pastry*
*6 oz flour*
*3 oz fat*
*4 oz soft margarine*

*Filling*
*4 oz caster sugar*
*2 eggs, beaten*
*2½ oz ground almonds*
*½ oz semolina*
*4 oz currants*
*2 oz peel*
*lemon water icing*

Make pastry with flour and fat and line 7 inch cake tin. Reserve a little for top.
Mix ground almonds and semolina.
Beat margarine and sugar until light and fluffy.
Add eggs carefully. Add ground almonds and semolina and fold in currants and peel. Cut remaining pastry into strips and make a trellis on top.
Bake at Gas 1-2/300°F/150°C.
Cover with lemon icing when cooled a little.
These can be made into small tartlets if preferred.

# ECCLES CAKES

*1 oz butter*
*2 oz brown sugar*
*1 oz candied peel*
*4 oz currants*
*nutmeg*
*approximately 6 oz of flaky pastry or shortcrust rolled out very thinly*

Melt butter in a saucepan and stir in brown sugar together with candied peel chopped very fine, currants and a little nutmeg. Do not allow to cook, just let the butter and sugar melt.
Roll out half flaky pastry and spread the mixture on top.
Cover with remaining pastry. Mark criss cross on top, allow currants to show through and sprinkle with sugar.
Bake in a moderate oven Gas 4/350°F/180°C.

# FLUFFY CAKES

*2 oz flour*
*1 teaspoon baking powder*
*6 oz cornflour*
*6 oz butter*
*4 oz caster sugar*
*2 eggs*
*little vanilla essence*

Sieve flour, baking powder and cornflour together. Mix with sugar.
Cream butter to light and fluffy stage and add gradually to the sieved ingredients.
Beat the eggs and add, and lastly a little vanilla essence.
Put in bun tins and bake in fairly hot oven for about 10 minutes.

# ALICE'S QUICK SHORTBREAD

*10 oz plain flour*
*2 oz farola*
*8 oz butter*
*4 oz caster sugar*

Beat butter and add sugar and other ingredients.
Roll out and cut into circles.
Cook at Gas 1-2/300°F/150°C until golden.

# FLORENTINES

This is one of the only recipes I use which is in new-fangled measurements and I always have to convert it back into imperial before I start. However, for the sake of progress I'm giving you the metric quantities!

*95 gm butter*
*100 gm caster sugar*
*100 gm flaked almonds*
*25 gm sultanas*
*25 gm glacé cherries*
*20 gm plain flour*
*100 gm plain chocolate*

Melt butter and add sugar. Boil for 1 minute. Add rest of the ingredients and put spoonfuls onto a greased baking sheet (lined with non-stick baking parchment). This quantity makes 12. Cook for 10 minutes Gas 4/350°F/180°C. Use a pastry cutter to tidy up the edges of each one, cool and coat with melted chocolate.

# MOGGY

From Yorkshire

*2 cups self-raising flour*
*1 cup soft brown sugar*
*4 oz margarine*
*2 tablespoons syrup*
*1 egg*
*1 teaspoon bicarbonate of soda*
*2-3 teaspoons ground ginger (add to taste)*

Put all ingredients in bowl and crack egg on top (mix slightly). Add a cup full of boiling water gradually – the mixture will be fairly soft. Put into a fairly deep rectangular tin and cook on the second shelf from the bottom of the oven for 1 hour. Gas 2/300°F/150°C.

# MARGARET'S MELTING MOMENTS

*5 oz self-raising flour*
*4 oz margarine*
*3 oz sugar*
*1 egg*
*cornflakes*
*vanilla*

Cream butter and sugar and add egg and flour together with cornflakes and a few drops of vanilla essence.
Make into rounds a little bigger than a walnut and put on greased baking tray.
Cook at Gas 1-2/300°F/150°C until golden brown.

# COCONUT OAT BISCUITS

*4 oz flour*
*4 oz coconut*
*2 oz lard*
*4 oz sugar*
*4 oz rolled oats*
*2 oz margarine*
*1 tablespoon golden syrup*
*2 tablespoons water*
*1 teaspoon bicarbonate of soda*

Mix the dry ingredients together and rub in the fat. Dissolve the bicarbonate of soda in the water. Mix in together with the golden syrup. Roll out on a floured board and cut into shapes.
Bake in a cool oven until nicely coloured.

**Handy hint**
*Use a plastic clothes peg to close a polythene bag with food in.*

# FREEZER CAKE

*8 oz butter*
*4 tablespoons syrup*
*1 packet shortbread biscuits*
*2 oz raisins*
*2 oz chopped nuts or ground almonds*
*8 oz chocolate*


Break biscuits into small pieces. Chop raisins. Melt butter with syrup and add biscuits, nuts and raisins and put into rectangular baking tray and cool. Cover with melted chocolate. Cut into small squares.


# LISA'S APPLE SPONGE

*8 oz butter or margarine*
*2 cups sugar*
*2 cups self-raising flour*
*4 eggs*
*4 large apples – peeled and sliced*
*almond essence*


Melt butter in saucepan. Add sugar and flour. Mix in eggs, apple and flavouring. Put into 2 greased and floured cake tins. Sprinkle with sugar. Bake Gas 6/400°F/200°C for ½ to ¾ hour. Serve warm with whipped cream.


*Freezer tips*
*Instead of putting a whole sponge cake in the freezer cut into portions separating with pieces of Bakewell under and up the sides of each piece to lift out easily.*

*Left over creamed potatoes can be piped into shapes for duchesse potatoes or baskets frozen and bagged, useful in an emergency.*

*Always double wrap grated cheese before freezing.*

# CHEESE SCONES

*6 oz self-raising flour*
*3 oz grated cheese*
*2 pinches cayenne pepper*
*1 oz butter*
*½ teaspoon mustard*
*1 egg and a little milk*
*½ teaspoon salt*


Rub flour and butter together.
Add cheese, mustard, salt and cayenne.
Beat egg and milk together in another basin, add to dry ingredients.
Roll out mixture (a softer mix than pastry) not too thin, cut out.
Coat with milk and put a little grated cheese on top.
Cook in a fairly hot oven. Gas 6/400°F/200°C.


# SISTER EVA'S SCONES

*4 oz flour*
*1 oz margarine*
*¼ teaspoon baking powder*
*¼ teaspoon cream of tartar*
*pinch of bicarb*
*pinch of salt*
*1 oz dates*
*1 oz grated chocolate*


Sieve all dry ingredients and mix to breadcrumb stage with margarine.
Add dates and chocolate and mix with sufficient milk to a softer consistency than pastry.
Cut into squares or rounds.
Cook at Gas 6/400°F/200°C for 10-15 minutes.

# SWEET OVEN SCONES

*12 oz self-raising flour*
*3 oz butter*
*2 oz sugar*
*milk to mix*


Make as before. These can be made with fruit if wished.


# MRS DODGSON'S OVEN SCONES

*8 oz self-raising flour*
*½ teaspoon bicarbonate of soda*
*½ teaspoon cream of tartar*
*2 oz lard*
*1 oz sugar*
*dried fruit (sultanas or currants as preferred)*
*pinch of salt*


Mix with milk a bit softer than pastry. Bake as for cheese scones.


# NORTHUMBRIAN PANCAKES

(Drop scones to the uninitiated)

*8 oz plain flour*
*1 teaspoon cream of tartar*
*½ teaspoon bicarbonate of soda*
*3 oz caster sugar*
*1 egg and milk to mix (a little more moist than pastry)*


Mix ingredients and drop spoonfuls on griddle. Should be eaten the same day.

# OATCAKES

*1 cup fine or medium oatmeal*
*1 teaspoon melted fat*
*1 pinch of bicarbonate of soda*
*1 good pinch of salt (to taste)*
*warm water to mix*


Mix everything together until mix is slightly sticky.
Using two boards roll out as thinly as possible with plenty of dry oatmeal to prevent sticking.
Turn on the boards and brush off the excess oatmeal with a pastry brush.
Cut off rough edges and put on a hot gridle 3½-4 minutes  whole, then cut into desired shapes.
Once the cakes begin to rise in the middle slightly or curl at the corners move to under the grill 2½-3 minutes until hard and curling at the edges.
NB: It is important to handle the mixture as quickly as possible, while still warm, when rolling out and in dry oatmeal.

# Preserves

Jams and chutneys are easy to make when the right ingredients are plentiful and it's a good way of capturing the fruits of summer. My method for jam making is dead simple and foolproof.

# ANNE'S JAM

*1 lb sugar*
*1 lb fruit*
*lemon juice*

Mix ingredients together in a large pan. Bring slowly to the boil and boil quickly for 4 minutes. Beat until set – I use my big mixer. Pot in the usual way.

# DRIED APRICOT JAM

A useful recipe if you feel like making jam and any other fruit is scarce.

*2 lb dried apricots*
*6 lb sugar*
*6 oz almonds*
*6 pints water*
*2 lemons*

Wash and soak the apricots for at least 24 hours. Put in a preserving pan with the water and simmer for 30 minutes. Add juice of lemons, sugar and almonds which have been blanched and shredded finely. Stir until sugar has dissolved. Boil quickly until setting point is reached. Pot in the normal way.

# LEMON CURD

*1 lb sugar*
*1 lb butter*
*3 lemons*
*4 eggs*

Heat sugar, butter, lemon juice and the grated rind of one of the lemons in a double boiler (or a basin over a pan of hot water) until dissolved. Beat and add the eggs and cook gently – still over hot water – until the lemon curd coats the back of the wooden spoon. Pot into small jars and cover.

# QUINCE JELLY

*4 lb quinces*
*6 pints water*
*sugar*

Wash the quinces, chop or mince and simmer with 4 pints water in a covered saucepan until tender. This will take about 1 hour. Strain through a jelly bag. Return pulp to pan with rest of water and simmer again. Strain this through a jelly bag. Mix the two extracts and measure. For each pint of juice add 1 lb of sugar. Bring to boiling point and boil rapidly until setting point is reached. Pot into warmed jars.

**Handy hint**
*Patterned material cut with pinking shears will make attractive covers for jars of jam and marmalade. Make a cardboard template first, using a jam pot cover and cutting approximately ½" larger.*

# REDCURRANT JELLY

Good with meats

*6 lb fruit – redcurrants or a mixture of red and white*
*sugar*

Place the cleaned fruit into a preserving pan and heat gently until the currants are tender. This will take about 45 minutes. Mash the fruit and strain through a jelly bag. Measure the juice and add 1¼ lb sugar to each pint. Bring to boiling point and boil for 1 minute. Skim the jelly and pour into warmed jars immediately. Cover in the usual way.

# THREE FRUIT MARMALADE

*2 grapefruit*
*4 lemons*
*2 sweet oranges*
*(total weight of fruit about 3 lb)*
*6 pints water*
*6 lb sugar*

Scrub and scald the fruit. Remove skins and some of the pith if very thick, and cut the rinds into shreds. Cut up rest of fruit coarsely. Put peel and half the water into a pan and simmer until peel is tender. Simmer rest of fruit and water for about 1½ hours and strain through a colander to remove pips. Add the pulp to the peel, bring to the boil and add the sugar, stirring until dissolved. Boil rapidly until setting point is reached. Remove scum, cool slightly and pour into warmed jars and cover in the normal way.

# SEVILLE ORANGE MARMALADE

*3 lb Seville oranges*
*6 pints water*
*6 lb sugar*
*juice of 2 lemons or 1 teaspoon citric or tartaric acid*

The method for this one is exactly the same as for the three fruit marmalade.

# VICTORIA PLUM CHUTNEY

*2 lb plums – stoned*
*1 lb onions – chopped*
*1 lb cooking apples – peeled and chopped*
*1 lb demerara sugar*
*8 oz red tomatoes – peeled and chopped*
*4 oz sultanas*
*1 pint malt vinegar (or more if necessary)*
*1 level tablespoon salt*

Mince plums, tomatoes, apples, onions and sultanas. Add with other ingredients to a large pan and simmer until well reduced. This will take 2½ or more hours. Pot in the usual way.

# RHUBARB CHUTNEY

2 lb rhubarb – chopped small
2 lb brown sugar
1 lb sultanas
2 lemons – peeled
1 oz garlic – finely chopped
1 oz root ginger – bruised
½ pint malt vinegar
¼ teaspoon cayenne pepper

Put ginger into a muslin bag and mix together with the other ingredients in a large pan. Simmer slowly for ½ to ¾ hour until it thickens. Remove ginger and pot.

# UNCOOKED APPLE AND DATE CHUTNEY

1 lb cooking apples
1 lb dates
1 lb onions
1 lb demerara sugar
1 pint vinegar
1 teaspoon salt
1 teaspoon dry mustard

Core and grate apples unpeeled. Chop onions and dates. Mix all other ingredients in a basin. Stand for 24 hours. Put through a food processor briefly to chop coarsely. Pot. This chutney keeps well despite being uncooked.

# TOMATO RELISH

*3 lb tomatoes – skinned*
*2 lb onions*
*1 lb sugar*
*1½ tablespoons dry mustard*
*1 tablespoon curry powder*
*vinegar*
*2 heaped tablespoons cornflour*

Chop tomatoes and onions, sprinkle with salt and leave overnight. Drain off water, put into pan and cover with vinegar. Boil for 5 minutes, then add mustard, curry powder and sugar. Boil for 30 minutes. Thicken with cornflour mixed with a little vinegar.

# TOMATO CHUTNEY

*1 lb apples*
*1 lb tomatoes*
*1 lb onions*
*1 lb sultanas*
*2½ lb brown sugar*
*¼ oz mustard seed*
*¼ oz ground ginger*
*a little cayenne pepper*
*lemon peel*
*1 tablespoon salt*
*vinegar*

Mince or chop the fruit and vegetables, cover with vinegar and simmer for 1 hour together with the spices and lemon peel. Add sugar and cook until thick. Pot.

# INDEX

# NOTES

# NOTES

# THE REDESDALE DAIRY

Makers of Speciality Farmhouse Cheeses from Cows, Sheep and Goats Milk

## Cheese Farm and Farm Shop

*Taste all our home-made cheeses and view the cheese-making room.*

*Home-made preserves, honey and other speciality foods.*

*Mail Order Service*

**Opening Hours**
Easter – October: 9.30–17.30
October – Easter: 9.30–14.30

**Soppit Farm, Otterburn, Northumberland NE19 1AF**
*Telephone: (0830) 20506    Fax: (0830) 20796*

(Two miles East of Otterburn on B6341, follow sign for Cheese Farm)

---

## *My Wine Merchant*

*For prompt, local, personal service and a range of wines from all over the world, individually chosen for their value for money and character then Simon Rowe is My Wine Merchant. He should be yours too!*

**My Wine Merchant**
**Tankerville Cottage Eglingham**
**Alnwick   Northumberland   NE66 2TX**
**Telephone: 0665 78 – 447**

- FRESH & FROZEN FARM MEAT - POULTRY AND FREE RANGE EGGS.
- HOME CURED BACON - FARM HOUSE BUTTER & CHEESE.
- HOME BAKING - JAMS & CHUTNEYS.
- FRESH FRUIT & VEGETABLES.
- LOCAL CARDS & GIFTS.
- MEALS AVAILABLE ALL DAY.
- SUNDAY LUNCH.
- LICENSED RESTAURANT.
- EVENING MEALS (RESERVATIONS ONLY)
- LOCAL CRAFTS.

# Roseden

## FARM SHOP RESTAURANT & PONY TREKKING

Five miles to the south of Wooler, "Gateway to the Cheviot Hills", Roseden Farm's fully licensed and approved trekking centre caters for experienced, beginners and disabled riders of all ages. Good basic instruction for beginners is supplemented by one or two hourly rides. Experienced riders can spend the day exploring the fields and forests of the Cheviot foothills or take a week-end break and enjoy 2 days trekking, together with dinner, bed and breakfast and a picnic lunch en route. Groups are well catered for too in the holiday cottage.

ROSEDEN · WOOPERTON
ALNWICK
Tel: (066 87) 271

# CP PRINTING & PUBLISHING LIMITED

*Kellaw Road, Yarm Road Industrial Estate, Darlington, Co. Durham DL1 4YA*
*Telephone: Darlington (0325) 382360*

# Also published by Bridge Studios

*Cooking with Love*
BBC MasterChef 1990 and cookery writer for *The Journal*, Joan Bunting
presents a delicious journey through the seasons of the year.    **Paperback £4.95**

*A Tune for Bears to Dance to*
Linda McCullough-Thew writes about her Northumbrian childhood. A
worthy successor to her first book *The Pit Village and the Store*.
**Paperback £5.95**

*Fifty Two Northumbrian Walks*
An account of some of the natural and historic attraction in a series of walks
written and illustrated by Ken Bunn.    **Paperback £4.95**

*Dark Tales of Old Newcastle*
A light-hearted look at some of the grimmer aspects of old Newcastle –
plagues and disasters, ghosts and witch-hunts and body-snatchers. Written
and illustrated by Pamela Armstrong.    **Paperback £2.95**

*Battle for Northumbria*
A graphic account of the battle and battlefields of Northumbria by John
Sadler.    **Paperback £6.95**

*Jack in the Navy*
*Jack in the Spirit*
*Back to the Pulpit*
A series of humorous tales of rural life from retired country parson Jack
Richardson aptly illustrated by Henry Brewis.    **Paperback £3.95**

*A Farmer's Lot...*
*Wild Oats and Wellingtons*
Two collections of humorous observations of life among farmers by journalist
Fordyce Maxwell.    **Paperback £3.95**

| | |
|---|---|
| *The Offishal Geordie Cook Book* | **Paperback £1.50** |
| *The Offishal Geordie Dictionarary* | **Paperback £1.50** |

**Bridge Studios**
**Kirklands**
**The Old Vicarage**
**Scremerston**
**BERWICK UPON TWEED TD15 2RB**

**Tel: 0289 302658/330274**